Woodpeckers to Helmets

Tech from Nature

By Jennifer Colby

21st Century
Junior Library

CHERRY LAKE
Publishing

Published in the United States of America by
Cherry Lake Publishing
Ann Arbor, Michigan
www.cherrylakepublishing.com

Reading Adviser: Marla Conn, MS, Ed., Literacy specialist, Read-Ability, Inc.
Content Adviser: Rachel Brown, MA, Sustainable Business

Photo Credits: © Martin Mecnarowski/Shutterstock.com, Cover, 1 [left]; © wavebreakmedia/Shutterstock.com, Cover, 1 [right]; © Hongqi Zhang (aka Michael Zhang)/Shutterstock.com, 4; © Mr.B-king/Shutterstock.com, 6; © arkanto/ Shutterstock.com, 8; © zeber/Shutterstock.com, 10; © Everett Collection/Shutterstock.com, 12; © Dana Gardner/ Shutterstock.com, 14; © Pete Wise/Shutterstock.com, 16; Public Domain/Wikimedia/Philip Henry Gosse [1849], 18; © Ronnachai Palas/Shutterstock.com, 20

Library of Congress Cataloging-in-Publication Data

Names: Colby, Jennifer, 1971– author.
Title: Woodpeckers to helmets / Jennifer Colby.
Description: Ann Arbor : Cherry Lake Publishing, [2019] | Series: Tech from nature | Audience: Grade 4 to 6. | Includes bibliographical references and index.
Identifiers: LCCN 2018035553 | ISBN 9781534142947 (hardcover) | ISBN 9781534139503 (pbk.) | ISBN 9781534140707 (pdf) | ISBN 9781534141902 (hosted ebook)
Subjects: LCSH: Helmets—Design and construction—Juvenile literature. | Woodpeckers—Juvenile literature. | Biomimicry—Juvenile literature.
Classification: LCC TP1185.H4 C65 2019 | DDC 391.4/3–dc23
LC record available at https://lccn.loc.gov/2018035553

Cherry Lake Publishing would like to acknowledge the work of the Partnership for 21st Century Skills. Please visit *www.p21.org* for more information.

Printed in the United States of America
Corporate Graphics

CONTENTS

Wear a helmet when riding a bike.

Staying Safe

Do you ride a bicycle? Maybe you have played on a football or baseball team. Wearing a helmet keeps you safe from harm.

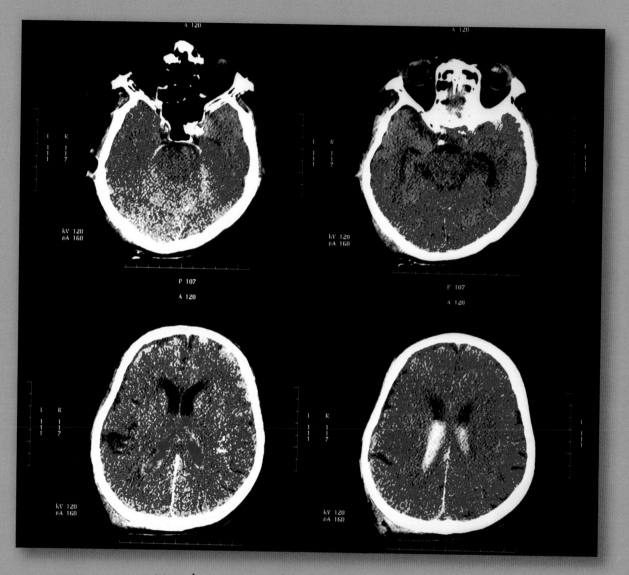

Your brain controls what your body does.

Protect Your Brain

People wear helmets to protect their heads while doing activities that could hurt them. Your head is one of the most important parts of your body. It's where your brain is! The brain is your body's computer. It controls how you breathe, think, and act. Injuries to your head can damage your brain. You could get a **concussion**.

There are many types of helmets.

Helmets have changed over the years. The study of woodpeckers has made helmets safer! How is this possible? Let's take a closer look at helmets.

Look!

Search around your home. How many types of helmets does your family own?

Early helmets were used for war and battles.
They were heavy and uncomfortable.

Helmets Throughout History

Helmets have been used for thousands of years. They were made to protect soldiers' heads during battles. Some were made from strong metals. Others were made of leather or thick cloth.

Helmets were used in sports in the 1800s. These simple helmets did little to protect the head. Then plastic was invented in the 1900s. Plastic helmets could protect the head from **impact**.

Before the 1900s, sports helmets were made of cloth and leather.

Modern helmets have a thick layer of foam on the inside. A thin layer of plastic covers the foam. Plastic is cheap and easy to **mold** into shapes. In 1940, plastic football helmets were designed. College and **professional** football players soon began wearing them.

The first plastic batting helmets for baseball were made in the early 1940s. These were hard and **durable**.

Plastic bicycle helmets were invented in the 1970s. These helmets were **lightweight** and more comfortable. They became popular with all types of cyclists.

Professional cyclists wear helmets when they race.

Today's helmets are much safer. New kinds of plastic are lighter and stronger. New foams can absorb harder hits.

But today's helmets are not perfect. People wearing them can still get a concussion. This is why it is so important to study nature. **Researchers** are studying the woodpecker to improve helmet safety.

Make a Guess!

Woodpeckers slam their beaks into wood at high speeds. How many times per second can a woodpecker peck? Write down your guess. Then read the next chapter. Was your guess close?

Woodpeckers peck trees to make nests or to find and store food.

Investigating Nature

Woodpeckers get their name from their habit of pecking holes into wood. Woodpeckers can peck about 20 times per second! They bang their heads about 12,000 times each day. These impacts are very powerful. Just one is more forceful than a hit that would cause a concussion in humans.

Scientists have learned that woodpeckers have spongy bones in their heads. These bones spread the force of a blow evenly around the body. Woodpeckers also have

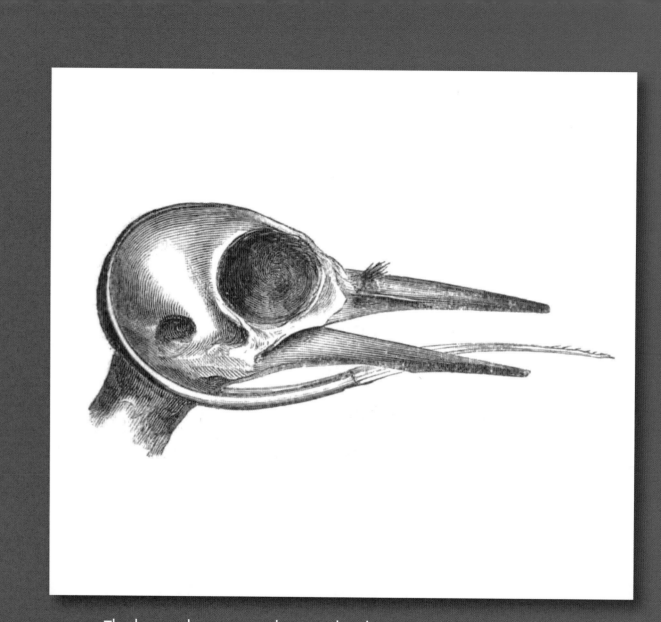

The bones that surround a woodpecker's tongue protect its brain.

flexible beaks. The top part of the beak is longer than the bottom half. When it slams into a tree, it bends down and back. This softens the blow of the impacts. This is why woodpeckers aren't hurt when they bang their head at powerful speeds.

A woodpecker's neck is extremely strong. The muscles in its neck absorb the shock of a peck. They transfer that shock to other

Think!

Do you use other protective gear for your activities? Maybe you use elbow pads, knee pads, or shin guards. Think about how these protect you from injury. Do you think they can be improved? How?

Wearing a helmet makes playing some sports safer.

parts of the body. Woodpeckers also have very long tongues! The extra bones that create space for the tongue **stabilize** the brain. This keeps a woodpecker's brain from sloshing around in its skull.

The study of woodpeckers has been useful in developing helmets. The design of new safety features copies the woodpecker's special **anatomy**. This is called **biomimicry**.

Ask Questions!

Think about other animals. Are there any that are similar to woodpeckers? What about animals with horns or shells? Ask a veterinarian or zookeeper how these animals protect their skulls!

GLOSSARY

anatomy (uh-NAT-uh-mee) the parts that form a living thing

biomimicry (bye-oh-MIM-ik-ree) copying plants and animals to build or improve something

concussion (kuhn-KUHSH-uhn) an injury to the brain that is caused by something hitting the head very hard

durable (DOOR-uh-buhl) staying strong and in good condition for a long time

impact (IM-pakt) the force of one thing hitting another

lightweight (LITE-wayt) not weighing very much

mold (MOHLD) to form or press into a particular shape

professional (pruh-FESH-uh-nuhl) making money for doing something that others do for fun, like sports

researchers (REE-surch-urhz) people who investigate a subject in order to find information

stabilize (STAY-buh-lize) to make something less easily moved

FIND OUT MORE

BOOKS

Rissman, Rebecca. *Should Henry Wear a Helmet?* Portsmouth, NH: Heinemann, 2015.

Statts, Leo. *Woodpeckers.* Edina, MN: ABDO Publishing Company, 2018.

WEBSITES

KidsHealth—Brain and Nervous System
https://kidshealth.org/en/parents/brain-nervous-system.html
This website explains the different parts of the brain and what they do.

National Geographic Kids—Pileated Woodpecker
https://kids.nationalgeographic.com/animals/pileated-woodpecker
Learn more about woodpeckers and then search this website for more information about other animals.

INDEX

ABOUT THE AUTHOR

Jennifer Colby is a school librarian in Ann Arbor, Michigan. She loves reading, traveling, and going to museums to learn about new things.